your 65th Birthday — April 13, 1983

Dear Daddy,

I hope you enjoy
this book. If it is hard
for you to read because of
your eye, let Mother read
it to you. I just wanted
to get you something special
on this day because you
are so special.

I love you so much.

PAT

Ten
Good
Things
I Know About
Retirement

Ten Good Things I Know About Retirement

J. WINSTON PEARCE

BROADMAN PRESS
Nashville, Tennessee

4254-29
ISBN: 0-8045-5429-2

Material on pages 2, 33, 65-66 from *Your Rewarding Years,* copyright © 1955, by Mrs. Clarence Hamilton, used with permission of the publisher, The Bobbs-Merrill Co., Inc.

Material on pages 49, 74-75 from *Green Winter* by Elsie Maclay is used with permission of the McGraw-Hill Book Company.

Material on pages 24, 45, 59, and 80 from *Going Like Sixty,* by Richard Armour is used by permission of Richard Armour.

Dewey Decimal Classification: 646.7
Subject heading: RETIREMENT

Library of Congress Catalog Card Number: 82-71668
Printed in the United States of America

To my sister
Violet
now a great-grandmother
who has stood on every rung of
life's ladder
and called it good

CONTENTS

INTRODUCTION

By the very ordering of nature and the universe, spring and summer exist for autumn. Everything worthwhile on this earth looks and moves toward fall. The final end and purpose of life is the harvest.

All is on the way to age, the golden fields, the creaking wagons and combines, the churning tractors, bulging barns, ripening orchards, gushing winepresses, the flowing cider. The preparing, planting, nursing, tilling, watching, and hoping are all in anticipation of fulfillment and completion. The simplistic and inclusive lines embrace the idea:

> Old wood is best to burn,
> . . . .
> Old friends to trust,
> And old authors to read.[1]

Let the lines stand, for an antidote is needed. Aging is usually presented as a horror story made up of loneliness, isolation, infirmities, poor housing, uselessness, and poverty. So vivid has this picture been focused on the screen of attention that we have scarcely been aware of the rewards of aging.

I do not deny that there is some basis for the

conventional view. However, I do affirm that it is not the total picture, nor does it present the facts and experience of most older people.

> The plain truth is that the overwhelming majority of old people in America are well, not sick. Most men and women over 65 can continue normal living; of the .15% who cannot, about one third are taken care of in institutions. On an average, old people spend less than fifteen days a year in bed due to illness . . . 80% of all aged say their health is excellent, good or fair . . . only 20% claim poor health.[2]

Eighty percent of old people live in their own homes or with relatives.[3] A young person is subject to a wider range of disorders than are the old. There are measles, mumps, whooping cough, and degenerative diseases that have a special affinity for the young. Also, serious difficulties are not as common among the elderly as with the young.[4]

As for social isolation, it may well be more apparent than real. Surveys indicate that most older people *prefer* separation from their children, the independence from ties that are too binding. A Lew Harris survey showed that 80 percent of older people who had children and were not living with them had seen the children within the past week, and more than half had seen them within the last day.[5]

Society tries to make too wide a distinction

between the person of thirty and that same person at the age of sixty-five. At age seventy-nine, J. B. Priestley, the English author, was asked, on the occasion of the publication of his ninety-ninth work, what it was like being old. He answered:

> It is as though walking down Shaftesbury Avenue as a fairly young man, I was suddenly kidnapped, rushed into a theatre and made to don the gray hair, the wrinkles and the other attributes of age, then wheeled on stage. Behind the appearance of age I am the same person, with the same thoughts, as when I was younger.[6]

There is the story of a man who wanted to become a bank director. The interested parties asked if he had ever served as a bank director. No, he never had. Had he ever worked in a bank? No, he never had. Did he major in banking when he was in college? No, he did not. Had he ever made any consistent effort to become knowledgeable in banking on his own? No, he never had done that. "Then, what," asked the interviewer, "do you think qualifies you to serve as a bank director?" The would-be bank director answered, "I was a depositor."

I am a depositor in this age bank. I retired ten years ago and am well past the biblical target of "threescore and ten" (Ps. 90:10). That may not be a full qualification for writing about aging, but it is a better qualification than that of many who do write about aging. For a careful check of publications reveals that most of the books and articles in magazines and journals, were written by younger people *about* older people. A large percentage of these books are not designed to help the elderly so much as to help others help the elderly.[7]

In the following pages I have sought to balance the books, to give the "pleasuring" retirees their long-delayed franchise. In doing so, I shall be making heavy withdrawals from my own age bank; after all, I am "a depositor." If in doing so the writing seems void of due modesty, I apologize. I have no desire to appear immodest but I do wish to communicate something of my gratitude for the years when the best wine (John 2:10) is being served. On his sixtieth birthday, Thornton Wilder received a cable from Justice Felix Frankfurter. It read, "Dear Thornton: Welcome to the great decade. Felix."[8]

P.S. One moment please. I almost forgot to say that the young have a special invitation to consider my testimony. For I remind them that "The time to economize on your sack of potatoes is when it is full. If you wait until you get to the bottom of the sack, it's too late to economize."[9]

1
PLEASURE
("Be a Courteous Guest in the
House of God")

"We are in the house of God," says a good and wise man, "and it is impolite not to take pleasure in what your host has to offer you; it is discourteous to the creator to reject the pleasures of life."[1]

Until I retired I felt almost apologetic about experiencing pleasure, joy, elation, or lightheartedness. I unconsciously had the impression that such emotions had to be *deserved* or *earned*. Pleasure was a side effect, a sort of serendipity for *positive* or *useful* deeds.[2] H. L. Mencken defined a puritan as a person who lived in mortal fear that somewhere, sometime, someone might enjoy himself."[3] And, while it may be that Mencken was incapable of understanding the Puritan Ethic, the caricature of the position has probably influenced our thinking about pleasure having its own voting rights.

But life is so constituted that to function properly, pleasure is a necessary ingredient for the good and healthy life. Norman Cousins, long-time editor of the *Saturday Review of Literature,* now senior lecturer at the School of Medicine, University of California at Los Angeles, wrote, *Anatomy of an Illness As Perceived by the Patient.* For months, the book remained on the best seller list. Commenting on that, Cousins said that he had written fourteen books, all on peace, national and international peace. Then, he wrote a book about his own personal illness and that book sold more copies than all his other books combined. Why? He said that he thought it was because people wanted to believe they were bigger than their problems.

Cousins was hospitalized in 1964 with a rare, crippling, incurable disease. He was aware of the power of negative emotions (noted in the last chapter). He wondered if positive emotions, pleasure, love, faith, hope, humor, a will to live, might be as helpful as negative emotions were harmful. He secured a movie projector, had it set up in his room, and obtained humorous films: *Candid Camera, The Marx Brothers,* and others. He sent friends to the libraries to search for books of humor. Then, he scheduled a time each day for fun and laughter, for belly laughs. Careful records were kept. The results were surprising. He found that for ten minutes of hearty laughter, he could get two hours of pain-free sleep. He checked the level of inflammation in his body following a laugh session; he and the medical team determined that there was a drop of about seven points. He discovered that laughter, joy, and pleasure, was a sort of anesthesia.[4]

James J. Lynch, noted psychologist, says that without love and companionship between husband

and wife, multitudes of persons in our country are prone to practically every major disease from mental illness to cancer. Pleasure and happiness are the keys to health and the substance of life.[5]

Pleasure causes one to feel young; misery makes one feel old. And, there is truth in the saying that you are as old as you feel. The wit, at least a half, who said that were it not for that he would be young. Auntie Mame, in Lawrence and Lee's drama of the same name, said that life was a banquet but most suckers were starving themselves to death.

I recall the story of the man who, when asked if his wife worked outside the home, answered, "I make the living and she makes the living worthwhile." Life as we know it has given us pleasure. Pleasure makes the free time worthwhile. My generation is the first to be forced to deal realistically with leisure, the first generation in history to spend more time in leisure than we spent in work. In 1870 the average work week was seventy hours; in 1900 it was fifty-five hours; today, it is thirty-eight hours. Working hours have decreased by three each decade since 1900. One of the major revolutions of our time is shifting from a work-oriented society to a leisure-directed one.[6] And, note this, 200 years ago, when the American republic was born, the average life expectancy for a man was thirty-three years; for a woman, thirty-five years. Today, both men and women may expect to live beyond their seventies.[7] Society and the overall circumstances of existence have added years to our lives. It remains for us to be sure that life is added to our years.

> If I grow older and do not know it,
> Immersed in sheer bliss,
> Perhaps I won't show it.[8]

But, "It ain't easy, McGee!" When I retired, I found that I was poorly prepared to deal with *myself*. I knew something about things; more about books; probably more, still, about people. But I had little experience in dealing with myself. Most of my professional life had been spent on "stage." I had been a salesman, a businessman, a minister, teacher, leader of seminars and conferences. I had practically no training for or experience with privacy. I did not know how to enjoy being alone. Yet, I knew that if I was to *enjoy* my retirement years I would have to learn to enjoy aloneness. There is neither profit nor pleasure in stuffing our leisure hours with activities merely for the sake of "killing time"—a tremendously apt phrase. As we were taught to work, how to work, when to work, and where, so, now, we need to know the same skill in leisure.[9]

Perhaps the experience of Abraham H. Maslow, the distinguished psychologist-philosopher, could be helpful. Dr. Maslow had a serious heart attack in his early sixties. He survived and expressed his pleasure in living and his joy at just being alive. In a tape that he sent his publisher just before his death in 1970 he said that his attitude toward life had changed. He thought of his existence now as "postmortem life." For, he might just as easily have died. He said that his living was something of an extra, a bonus given to him, and that it was all gravy! Everything, now, was doubly precious to him. He said that he was stabbed by such things as flowers, babies, and beautiful things. He said the very act of living, of breathing, of walking, of eating, having friends, talking, everything, everything looked so beautiful![10] "Only the old are capable of savoring pleasure soberly, thoroughly and with complete absorption."[11]

Pleasure, "pleasuring," does not lie primarily in our surrounding or in our activities, or the lack of activities. It lies basically in ourselves. Pleasure, or its lack, is determined by our response to the experiences that we face, whether those experiences be good or bad, hard or comfortable. It is not necessary for all of life to be good in order to find pleasure in the parts of life that are good. We do not have to be free of pain constantly to enjoy the freedom when it arrives. It is not essential that every part of the body be strong to be thankful for those parts of the body that are strong. Everything is not bad just because a few things are not good.

Remember, "We are guests in the house of God, and it is impolite not to take pleasure in what your host has to offer you: it is discourteous to the creator to reject the pleasures of life."[12]

2
FREEDOM
(It Is "A Universal License to Do Good")

On the day he retired, Horace Whittell, Gillingham, England, brought to work the alarm clock which had roused him at six o'clock for forty-seven years. He placed the clock on the concrete, climbed into an eighty-ton press, and roared over the infernal noisemaker. He said, "It was a lovely feeling!"

Freedom is a lovely feeling. We come into life seeking it. I observed the quest in the lives of my own children. A few hours after each child was born, the search began. Those kids kicked and screamed at every restraint. They wanted out of the bed, out of the playpen, out of the nursery room, out of the house, out of the yard, out of the playground.

The search continued. The children were convinced that if they could just get away from home, freedom would be theirs. They would find it in kindergarten, later in grade school, then in high school, surely in college. No? Then it would certainly be theirs when they got the first job, when they had their own families. On and on the search continues. Yet, with each step up the ladder of life, on to retirement, freedom becomes more and more that will-o'-the-wisp. The search continues throughout life. The more successful we become, the less freedom is allowed us. The type of responsibilities may change but there is no diminution of restraint. The "fleas come with the dog," as the old adage states it.

Then comes age and retirement! One of the first pleasures I experienced in retirement was freedom. Not absolute freedom, of course, we never reach that, fortunately. But, there is more freedom than was ever experienced before. Three years after he retired, a friend said to me, "Winston, do you know what I like about being retired? If there's anything I've got to do, I don't have to do it!" You might polish his grammar; I doubt you could improve on his sentiment.

The alarm clock can be crushed; the traffic jams can be avoided; the time clock does not have to be punched; the sales schedules and calendars can be ignored, class assignments, the grading of papers, and the posting of grades no longer make demands upon us. In terms of school, you now have, finally, academic freedom. And that means, according to one sharp observer: freedom from ultraconservative trustees, freedom from ultraliberal faculties, and freedom from ultrademanding students.[1]

Years ago I succeeded Dr. John Henry Day as minister of the historic Seventh Baptist Church in Baltimore. Dr. Day had retired after a long and distinguished career. A few weeks after I arrived an important committee meeting was scheduled. I felt that Dr. Day's long years with the church would give him knowledge and experience that the group needed. So, I invited him to meet with us. He said, "No, Pearce, I will not come to that committee meeting. I wish you well but I shall not attend. "And," he added with a puckish grin, "I'll tell you something; when I die, if I am invited to a committee meeting, I shall know that I have gone to the wrong place!" Freedom.

The freedom that we seek, and within bounds find, is not just freedom *from*, it is freedom *to and for*. We go not into a vacuum but into more desirable and interesting activities and engagements; we go to these activities, these pleasures, at our own pace and standard of quality.

Our priorities change. That is, it is best that our priorities change; it is essential that our priorities change; it is *imperative* that our priorities change! This has been true at every advancing level of life. The priorities for the teen years are different from those of childhood. The young adult cannot live successfully on the priorities of the teens. The businessman, the responsible executive, the accountable professional person has to have a different set of priorities. Of course, in retirement, our priorities change. It is important that we change them for ourselves rather than having others change them for us. Why hold onto, or relinquish with regret, that trip on ulcer lane, or that drive on high blood pressure thoroughfare! Let others have the responsibility and burdens of the "rat race" and the "dog fight." As Peter Schwed says, "When you give up power and authority, you also give up the headaches, the pressures, and the ulcers that so frequently go with it . . . the bus is much less crowded in the rear."[2]

Freedom in retirement comes not through avoiding all responsibility, but through shucking those obligations that were required of us in mid life. This makes it possible to assume the assignments that are appropriate to and commensurate with our senior years. Responsibilities carried over from one stage of life into a later stage is what disrupts the flow of growth and enjoyment in the retirement years. The old Shaker verse is apropos:

> Leave the flurry
>   To the masses;
> Take your time
>   And shine your glasses.[3]

3
LOVE
(It Causes the Sun to Rise in the West!)

I have seen the following statistics, not sure who ran the survey. Three percent of the American people are highly successful; 68 percent are moderately successful; 29 percent are total failures. Where would you place yourself? Just hold that question, and your ready(?) answer, in abeyance, for a moment.

I have had five distinct careers. The list includes being a businessman, a pastor of churches, a teacher in graduate schools, and a writer. To the best of my ability to evaluate, in each of those professions I should be placed in the 68 percentile, among the moderately successful persons. I certainly could not place myself in the 3 percentile group of highly successful persons. I honestly do not think my place is among the total failures. I was moderately successful in business, in the pastorate, in teaching, and in writing.

That lists four careers. I claim a fifth. And the fifth profession has elicited my interest and concern as none of the others have. I have worked at it longer and have pursued it with greater enthusiasm. It is my candid opinion that I have been more successful with it, and paradoxically, failed more miserably in pursuing it.

That career? Husband and lover. That is my fifth and preferred vocation. I have followed it for forty-five years. That is, I have followed it for forty-five years if you keep the "husband and lover" joined. If you separate the two, a few years have to be added!

Now for a personal declaration. I would rather be highly successful as husband and lover than to attain that lofty height in any other profession. I do not give that evaluation lightly, nor have I always reached that appraisal. I have had as much ambition to succeed in each of the other four careers as the law ought to allow. I wanted to be highly successful in everything I did. Still, today, if a choice had to be made, I would choose to be highly successful as a husband and lover.

This assessment comes only with age, for most persons. It takes a long time to be married. It does not take long to get married. Nor does it take an extended period of time to fall in love. It takes much time for two individuals to become loving. That is something which has to be learned; it requires time, patience, and discipline. It is a lifetime undertaking, and we get no time off for good behavior.

I am joyfully convinced that only those who have endured and come to the retirement years can know the pleasure, rewards, and ecstacy of married love. When Robert Bridges, poet laureate of England, came to write of married love in the senior years, he drew a comparison between love in youth and love in age. He wrote that love in youth was like a small stream while love in age was a wide and flowing river. He affirmed that now when he was basking in "love complete," he found himself wondering "how love so young could be so sweet." Bridges was eighty when he wrote that.[1]

In retirement years, I have relearned the joys and rewards of dating, those choice times when the concern of each is for the happiness of the other. It is the time of the treasured perfume, the favorite flower, the preferred dress, the admired suit and tie, the special restaurant, and the carefully planned conversation, allowing only talk that is pleasing to the companion. This is to follow the procedure known in the early days of dating. But there is a difference now. With the renewed interest in, knowledge of, and love for each that the years have brought, the whole dating experience is vastly enhanced.

In retirement, the sphere of romance and sex takes on new beauty. Who was it made the saucy observation that there were two kinds of people in the world, those who were interested in sex, and liars! That is probably more pertinent than the remark of the stooped and bitter old centenarian who, after having heard a rousing sermon on the "sex revolution," wheezed to his minister, "Parson, just where was that sex revolution when I was able to rebel!" The French writer, Bernard Fontenelle, a friend of Benjamin Franklin, said to fabulous Madam Helvetius, "Ah, my dear, if I were only ninety again!" He was one hundred; she was sixty.[2]

The senior years are when romance and sex come to culmination. And, if the young wish to argue, the cliché is in order, "Don't knock it until you've tried it!" The beauty, tenderness, understanding, meaning, and skill of a lifetime can now be brought to the bower of love. Barbara Cartland, the successful writer of romantic novels, after half a century at her craft, says that love is an art and the more one practices it, the better it gets.[3] Of course! And when a man and a woman, within the bonds of marriage, have had the courage, loyalty, fidelity, manhood, and womanhood to meet and to satisfy the romantic and sexual needs of each other for a lifetime, they and, probably, they alone, qualify for the accolade "great lovers!"

It is in the retirement years that a man and a woman come to know and appreciate qualities in each other that can neither be revealed nor comprehended in earlier years of marriage. In her helpful book, *Your Rewarding Years,* Mrs. Clarence H. Hamilton recounts the experience of a friend. The friend and her husband had lived a busy life, raised a large family of children, and now they were in retirement. Surprises! The friend said that in the earlier years of their marriage she and her husband had never talked; they had no time for it. Of course, they had discussed household things, the children, the husband's work, and financial problems. But they had never talked about things that concerned just the two of them. She said, almost in amazement, "We're learning all sorts of fascinating things, catching up on what we missed before. . . . I had no idea Joe could be so good a conversationalist. I'm proud of him! Everybody listens when he talks!"[4] There are your "acres of diamonds" found in your own backyard (spouse) that Russell Conwell spoke so enthusiastically about.

Professor Halford Luccock once wrote that the most beautiful tribute ever paid to marriage was spoken by Humpty Dumpty in *Alice Through the Looking Glass.*[5] Recall that Humpty Dumpty was unhappy because Alice was growing so fast. Alice informed him that she did not seek advice about growing because one couldn't help growing old. To which Humpty Dumpty replied, "One can't, perhaps, but two can." I like that! Almost as much as I like Brickman's cartoon, "The Small Society." A man asks an older couple what, in the light of the crazy inflation, are they going to hold on to. The answer: "To each other."

4

HOBBIES

(One a Day Keeps the Blues Away)

"No man is really happy or safe without a hobby," wrote Sir William Osler, the distinguished teacher-physician.[1] It was only in retirement that I was able to test Dr. Osler's dictum. Earlier, there was no time to "dust my bells" and ride away to whatever tune I pleased, or that pleased me.[2]

From the beginning of my professional life, I was *interested* in hobbies. This is how and where and when and with whom it started. It was at the regular weekly meeting of my Rotary Club, a time to eat and talk and yawn as some ordinary person delivered a very ordinary address, on a very ordinary ragamuffin day. So I thought, but I was in for a surprise. The speaker was Dr. George B. Cutten, president emeritus of Colgate University. His subject was "My Hobby." Early American silver was his special interest. His expertise in the field had resulted in his publishing three books on the subject. As he spoke to us, his enthusiasm ran at high tide; he was like a small boy with his gifts on Christmas morning! Listening to him, sensing his excitement, I wanted to be old enough to retire that very day!

Hobbies are chosen in different ways—or, hobbies choose persons in different ways, if you prefer. What has been an avocation before retirement may become a hobby that is close to a second vocation in retirement. What has been a vocation in life may become an eagerly pursued hobby in retirement. More frequently, however, the hobby that claims an individual in retirement is a new interest, at least an interest that one was unable to follow earlier for lack of time and freedom.

That is the case with one of my favorite hobbies, reading. The two careers that claimed most of my professional life, ministry and teaching, demanded that I read much. However, my reading in retirement is quite different. The content of the reading is different and my purpose is not the same. Earlier, I read to keep "intellectually respectable" in my chosen fields of work. Now, my reading is for enjoyment, pure and simple. If I do not find pleasure in the reading, the book is usually put down.

Recently, I discovered a new author. Why I had missed her for so long, I do not know. Having made the discovery, I sought to rectify my shortcomings without delay. What a treat! A half hundred books bear her name as author. One entire winter and a large part of spring were brightened by her stimulating characters and intriguing plots. The reading gave me new friends, as real as the neighbor next door. It gave me sheer delight and, make no mistake at this point, *delight,* pleasure, is an essential of successful living. The reading put truth and virtue into flesh and blood and I saw those two principles in action. In my reading I received inspiration. I saw men and women face hardship and disappointment with courage and fortitude until I dared believe that I could act in such a way if called upon to do so!

In his delightful *The Haunted Bookshop,* Christopher Morley has the old bookman say that it is a source of great sorrow to him that he will die with so many wonderful books unread. Then he makes a confession. He has never read Shakespeare's *King Lear*. His reason for not reading that masterpiece? If the time ever came when he was very ill and the doctors were very sure that he was going to die, all he would have to do would be to say to himself, "Hey, you can't die; you haven't read Lear!" The old man was very sure that such a reminder would bring him around! Great![3]

Travel stands high on my list of hobbies. Travel is costly and that has to be considered by most retirees. It certainly is a consideration for the Pearces. Drawing heavily upon my own observation and experience, let me suggest this. It does not cost as much to travel at home as it does to travel abroad. And, very few of us have reaped the full benefit of travels at home. And, if there is something or someone of significance in the next state, county, or town, it may be as important that you travel there as that you go to Europe next summer.

As for traveling at home, it, too, is costly. However, there are considerations. The time, the place, the mode of travel have much to do with prices. Those of us who are retired are doing a great percentage of the traveling these days. Our business is important; we are catered to; reductions are freely offered. There are many ways to economize.

The Pearces often travel with friends by car. And, tongue in cheek, I report on one way the four of us cut expenses. We found that the four of us, two couples, needed only one motel room with two double beds. When friends raise an eyebrow at that and ask if it is not embarrassing when we go to bed, I answer, "No, we learned that if we took off our bifocals, there were no problems."

Cicero, the Roman orater wrote, "If the soul has food for study and learning, nothing is more delightful than an old age of leisure." What goes on in the mind and heart of the individual is more important for one than what goes on in one's environment.

> My mind to me a kingdom is;
> Such present joys therein I find
> That it excels all other bliss
> That earth affords or grows by kind.[4]

The entire field of interest and learning is of crucial importance in the retirement years. As we become less active physically in retirement, we can become more alert mentally. There is additional time for growth of mind and soul. Opportunity abounds to revel in the riches of the ages. That which has inspired and enlightened others has been recorded; we can read, think, apply, and make our own.

One of the first calls made by President Franklin Roosevelt following his inauguration was to see Justice Oliver Wendell Holmes, Jr. Justice Holmes was ninety-two. The President found the Justice in his library reading Plato. "May I ask why you are reading Plato, Mr. Justice?" asked Roosevelt. "Certainly, Mr. President. To improve my mind."[5]

At age seventy-five, my sister, a mother, grandmother, and a great-grandmother, enrolled for study in a theological seminary. For years, she had taught a Bible class in her church. She wanted to be a better teacher and now she had time to study. She profited from the experience and made excellent grades. She allowed me to read one of her final examination papers. At the close of the paper, I saw the words written by her professor, "You have been an inspiration to the class."

It has been observed that the happiest people are those who touch life at the greatest number of points. My own life is enriched by having a number of hobbies. The field is wide: auctions, autograph collecting, baking, bird watching, animals, coin collecting, hiding-out, drawing, painting, fishing, stamp collecting, writing, window-shopping. John Warren Steen tells about a retiree living in Georgia who, when asked what he had done in life that he was proud of, answered, "I've turned in three fire alarms, none false."[6]

One of my hobbies is fishing. When I retired, I resolved that I would fish one half day each week. I have to admit that I have not done that. I have fished one full day each week! Izaak Walton wrote, "I have laid aside business, and gone a-fishing." And, to justify his action, he added, "We may say of angling as Dr. Boteler said of strawberries: 'Doubtless God could have made a better berry, but doubtless God never did'; and so, if I might be judge, God never did make a more calm, quiet, innocent recreation than angling."[7]

A hobby a day may not keep the doctor away from your retirement domicile but it is a better and more potent medicine than that proverbial apple!

5

WORK

(It "Ain't Unless You'd Rather Do Something Else")

I have found that work is one of the good things about retirement. Of course, there is work in retirement. George Bernard Shaw gave it as his opinion that "A perpetual vacation is a good working definition of hell."[1] And Richard Armour smilingly agrees,

> Retired is being tired twice, I've thought:
> First tired of working, then tired of not.[2]

But there are three differences in work before and after retirement. First, in retirement, you are able to do what you want to do. There are those who were fortunate enough to do that before retirement. Truthfully, I was in that group. Yet, there are many who always hated the work they were required to do. Early in life they were caught in it. Heritage, immediate family responsibilities, depression times, lack of other advantages; one of these, a combination, or for other reasons they were never able to free themselves. So, from the beginning they went to their work like quarry slaves scourged to their dungeons, as William Cullen Bryant put it.[3]

I have a friend who spent most of his working years in the automobile business. He was highly successful, became a millionaire, and had the respect of his peers. He retired recently. In conversation, I complimented him on his successful career. He dismissed a lifetime of work with one sentence: "I never liked it." Sad. But now in retirement he can, and is, doing what he wants to do.

I admit there are limiting factors. One can seldom do absolutely and without restraints just what one may want to do. Recently, after giving an address on retirement in which I stressed the point that in retirement you had the freedom to do just what you wanted to do, two elderly women approached me. One said, "You know, I am not that old, yet. I still can't do just what I want to do." The second lady said, her words accompanied by an amused grin, "Well, my case is different. I am past the age when I can do just what I want to do!" Both cases understood. Still, within reasonable bounds, you can do in retirement what you want to do.

Second, in retirement I have found that I not only can do what I want to do, I can do it the way I want to do it. That is important. The degree of freedom allowed persons in the work they do varies with the person, the type of work, and the circumstances under which the work is performed. However, it can be safely stated that a person is seldom able to do one's work just the way one would like to do it. There are production schedules, sales quotas, competition, reputation, standards, etc. In retirement most of these restrictions are lifted. You can do your work as you wish to do it.

Basically, there are only two requirements. One, you fulfill, to the best of your ability, the requirements of God. Second, you meet, as you are able, the demands of your own conscience—it may be that for you the two merge into one. After these two requisites have been given space, you can do your work as you desire to do it. You can look the job and the supervisor eyeball to eyeball and say, gently, of course, "You have nothing that I need or desire that would cause me to do this job differently from the way I really want to do it."

Rudyard Kipling wrote a poem about earth's last picture. He said that in painting that final picture, no one would work for money and no one would work for fame but that each would work for the joy of the working and that each would draw the thing as he saw it.[4] We approach that ideal in retirement. At the age of eighty, Rubinstein, the pianist, was told that he was playing better than ever. His response is significant:

> Now I take chances I never took before. You see, the stakes are not so high. I can afford it. I used to be so much more careful. No wrong notes. Not too bold ideas . . . Now I let go and enjoy myself. . . .[5]

Third, I like work in retirement because I can do it *when* I want to do it. I do not have to punch a time clock, nor do I have to stop when a certain whistle blows. If I wish I can work all night, for I can sleep the next day. Or if I wish, I can skip a day, a week, or longer, and pick up the job when more important things like fishing or reading that good book have been given satisfaction. "Old age," wrote Somerset Maugham, "is ready to undertake tasks that youth shirked because they would take too much time."[6] Right. Youth has to finish one job and hurriedly get to another in order that the production schedule be kept up in order, that the paycheck may come in on time so that the bills can be paid the first of the month.

Given these three differences in work before and in retirement, what, how, and when, it should not be surprising that much of the world's creative and lasting work is done in the retirement years. If a person can do what one wants to do, do that work in the way one wants to do, do the work when one wants to do it, the results can be gratifying and significant.

Shortly after I retired, the president of Campbell University and the board of trustees asked me to write the history of the school. Immediately, one of the above guidelines was met. I wanted to write the history of Campbell University, for the institution had meant much to me and to my family. I asked the second question, "May I do the work as I want to do it?" I was assured that I could, that it would be so stated in the contract. Then the third question, "May I do the writing when I want to do it?" I was guaranteed that the time schedule would be of my own choosing. With that understanding, I went to work. The writing was a delight and a fulfilling experience.

Elise Maclay has a retired carpenter to say:

> I like to make things out of wood.
> The older I get, the stronger I build.
> Am I trying to build immortality?
> I don't think so.
> I know that whether I live or die
> The things I make have a life of their own,
> Separate and apart.
> I just want them to have a good life
> And long,
> Like I've had.
> Thanks, God, for building me strong.[7]

There is, it seems to me, another reason why a person's best work is often done in retirement. The reason was suggested above. In retirement, the financial consideration need not loom so large. It is surprising how much more freedom one feels once the financial incentive has been removed. I like the story of the doctor, well into retirement, whose telephone rang in the middle of the night. A neighbor wanted the retiree to come over to see his wife who was ill. The doctor asked the neighbor if he was able to pay for his services. Indignantly, the neighbor replied that, of course, he could and would pay. "Then, you had better call on one of the young doctors. I am too old to go out at night to see someone who is able to pay."[8] Wow!

But if you want to send the bill, by all means do so. Garson Kanin writes about the town that had a blackout. All effort to get the power plant back in operation failed. Finally, someone remembered an old retired engineer who had worked at installing the power plant. He was sent for and came. The old man made a careful examination of the electric centers, took a small mallet from his pocket and tapped a certain switch. The power came on; the crisis was over. Later, the town received the following bill:

For tapping	$ .02	
For knowing where to tap	$1,000.00	
Total		$1,000.02.[9]

John Ciardi stated the case in verse:

The old crow is getting slow.
The young crow is not.

Of what the young crow does not know
  The old crow knows a lot.

At knowing things the old crow
  Is still the young crow's master.
What does the slow old crow not know?
  How to go faster.

The young crow flies above, below,
  And rings around the slow old crow.
What does the fast young crow not know?
  Where to go.[10]

P.S.: Did you see the delicious quote from Horace Mann? "I have never seen," he wrote, "anything about the resolutions of the disciples, but a great deal about the acts of the apostles."

6
FRIENDSHIP
(You Prune, Perfect, and Plus It)

In retirement I have sought to do three things in the realm of friendship. First, I have trimmed the roster. During my earlier years, the list of those called "friends" had grown and grown and grown. There were business and professional associates, civic confederates, social sidekicks, educational partners, and religious co-workers. Some of these were above, some below, and some way out from me in terms of ideals, goals, and life-style. I owed favors to many of these. In order to accomplish what I considered worthy ends it was essential that we work closely together and to present a united front. We were "friends." Now, those restraints are loosed. So far as presenting a front of "friendship," I can, and am, free of the whole "kit and caboodle" of them. Lawrence Peter once gave three categories of friends: best friends, guest friends, and pest friends.[1] I have pared my roster of "pest friends."

Second, I have majored on, much more so than before, those old friends who are a pleasure to be with. I have tried to practice Shakespeare's precept: "Those friends thou hast, and their adoption tried/Grapple them to thy soul with hoops of steel."[2] I learned during my professional life that it was difficult to cultivate and keep in good repair quality friendships. If that seems questionable, ask yourself, "How many close, quality friends do I have who were my close friends forty years ago?" Love frequently demands less than friendship. Friendship, like fire, oftentimes goes out when unattended.

In retirement, there is time to enhance the quality of relationships with friends. I do it through reminiscing. I like to remember an old friend, when and how we met, how the friendship grew, experiences that we shared, laughter we have known, travels we have enjoyed, tasks that we mutually undertook. Kahlil Gibran says that a friend is your need answered.[3]

Letters, telephone calls, and personal visits play a prominent part in my cultivation of old friends. Recently my wife and I had a telephone conversation with a close friend. While circumstances had put distances in our togetherness, the bonds still held. We were informed in that telephone conversation that she was within 250 miles of us, would be there thirty-six hours, but would be unable to visit us. Immediately, we made plans to join her and to have five enriching hours together.

Two years ago, we did not send Christmas cards. As cards came from friends and acquaintances, we filed the greetings carefully. On the first day of January, we began to answer the cards with letters, supplementing the cards received with our own carefully built-up list of names. We continued the process; some days we wrote as many as five letters. If we were unable to write on a particular day, we were careful to see that we wrote a minimum of two letters the next day—some of these were brief, personal notes, some were lengthy, newsy letters of gratitude. In late October we came to the end of what had proved a delightful experience that had resulted in the cementing of friendships.[4]

The Pearces are members of a birthday dinner group that meets once each month. Ten times each year we meet in the homes of members. Twice each year we go out to fine restaurants. This group has met monthly for almost half a century. Remember the song, "Every Face Tells a Story"? As I look into the faces of these friends whom we hold so dear, it seems that whatever life has to bestow, good or bad, joy or sorrow, one or another of these friends has experienced it. These experiences have been shared with each other. And, by every occurrence, we have been drawn closer and closer together. Whenever we meet, the sentence is picked up and carried forward. We never use periods; only commas and exclamation points; now and then a question mark. Then when we meet the friendship moves forward.

And, there are new friends. In retirement, there is time to make new friends. And, I find it is easier to cross lines in making new friends. As indicated, in my professional life, there was time and opportunity only for those of my peer group. These were the persons I saw, was with in work; there was little time to go beyond that. Now, the lines are more blurred. I live in a university community and it is, of course, easy and natural to make new friends here as, each year, we have a covey of new faces on the faculty and administrative rosters. It is a great group, wonderful friends in the list. But in retirement I have time to make new friends among the maintenance crew, keepers of the golf links, farmers, and grove people. These have added zest to my daily experience.

And children. Some of my finest friends are among the very young. Yesterday morning, I took a nine-year-old boy fishing. He didn't know how to bait a hook, cast a line, or reel in a fish. Yet, he caught a dozen beautiful bream. Before we came in, I gave him a turn at steering our motor-driven canoe over the lake. As I took him home he said, shyly, "We'll have to do this again."

Mark Twain once wrote that he did not like to commit himself about heaven and hell for he had friends at both places. Probably, we all could say the same. But the friends I have in the here and now are something to smile about:

> Old friends, I've heard it said, are best,
> Which seems unfair to all the rest.
> For instance, friends I've met just now
> All these years I've missed somehow.
> I couldn't help it, nor could they,
> We didn't meet until today.
> Friends old or new I find so great
> I never check the starting gate.[5]

There is another friendship that I am developing in retirement, friendship with my wife! Love? Oh, yes, we have kept that healthy and growing. In the kingdom of friendship, we have more to learn. Dr. Samuel Southard has a thoughtful book with the interesting title, *Like the One You Love*. In "like" or friendship, he means the enjoyment that is found in doing things together, in mutual respect and fulfillment. He thinks of "love" as being more closely associated with sentimentality, sexual attraction, the giving and receiving of affection.[6]

To live with a person for many years in the relationship of husband and wife and then discover that your spouse is not only a wonderful lover, wife, and mother, but that she measures up in every way as your best friend. To discover after the good years together that there are areas of interest, insight, knowledge, humor, spirit of adventure, that are new, or have depths, that you never knew.

Oh, yes, one of the great needs of friendship in marriage was stated by someone with a mischievous grin on his face, I feel sure. He said it was possible to always tell a real friend because when you had made a fool of yourself he or she did not feel that you had done a permanent job. And our old friend "Anon" affirms that "A true friend will see you through when others see that you are through."

7
CHILDREN
(In Praise of the Empty Nest)

There are those who doubt that parents can ever *like* their children as long as they are at home. You *love* your children, of course, but like? Like calls for comparisons, for evaluations, for careful assessment. The paternal and filial relationships do not lend themselves to these procedures.

Children know exactly where we tie our goats and how to get to them! We feel so responsible when the children are at home: what they do and what they do not do, what they know and do not know, where they go and do not go. The responsibility bug continues to bite and sting. In one of Hank Ketchum's delightful cartoons, Dennis is asked what he is going to be in life if the neighbors let him grow up! Parents, as well as "Mr. Mitchell," sometimes wonder.

Then comes the "empty nest" stage. The children leave home for college, jobs, and their own homes and families. It was at this stage that I began to take a calm and careful look at my children. I began to see them not just as "brats," as "kids," but as persons, individual persons. I was able to compare them with other young people. I was able to evaluate their character, talents, and achievements. I learned that I had done a better job of parenting than I had thought! Wonderful discovery!

I was teaching in Switzerland. And, at Christmastime, one of our daughters and her family came over to be with us for the holidays. Within a few short hours that daughter was a vital part of our international student community. It was as if she had been there for months. She came with ease, grace, poise, enthusiasm, and with humor. Her mother and I were pleased, also surprised. I had known that she was an exceptional person, of course she was; she was her mother's daughter, graduate of a fine university, and a competent high school teacher. But to see her perform in that cosmopolitan academic setting was new. When she left, I said to her mother, "She really is a remarkable young woman!" Now, I could not see that when she was living at home. It took time, maturity, and a degree of objectivity not available to me in the earlier passage of life.

And this needs to be added. The growth and understanding is not all on the part of parents. The children see us in a new light. Recall the frequently quoted remark attributed to Mark Twain. He said that when he was fourteen years old his old man was so ignorant that he could hardly stand him, but by the time he reached twenty-one, he was amazed at how much his old man had learned!

Here is a perceptive and revealing message

taken from a daughter's letter to her parents shortly after they had visited in the daughter's home:

It is your generation which is making an art of living and really enjoying life. That's what we are looking forward to. And that's why I think we need settled and serene old age around us in quantity, so we can catch some of its essential ingredients, by osmosis or contagion, or something.

It's the feeling we got from your visit, brief as it was. You came into our normally frantic scene, and calmness and dignity and settledness walked right in with you. To you it probably seems as if you were walking into our atmosphere, but to us, we feel your atmosphere coming in—a kind of serenity we've never felt we had time to create. And just since your visit, our new house has felt more like a home, instead of a project, if you know what I mean. Seeing you, and having you both so very much the same as always, the way you look and talk and do things, that's the kind of unchangingness we all need.

I haven't felt impatient any more to get rid of that miserably uncomfortable chair in the living room, ever since Dad sat there reading that day, looking so comfortable and the same old Dad. Now the old chair seems to belong to the stable familiar, and we'll part with it rather sadly when the time comes. But we'll probably follow Art's suggestion and get the new one just before your next visit, so you can work your magic on it.

> The kids need more of their grandparents.
> . . . They've talked of nothing else since you left
> and are planning ahead for your next visit.[1]

In retirement, one of our great interests is in our children and our grandchildren. We do not feel the *responsibility* for their development and welfare that we once felt. But our *desire* for their welfare is not less. Could it be that now, in the retirement years, we can make our most vital contribution to their lives? If so, we shall make it in two directions.

First, we shall make it in revealing, through living, the happiness and the fulfillment that we have discovered in our marriage and home life. While preparing for her wedding, one young woman was overheard to say to a friend, "I only hope I can have as wonderful a marriage as Mother and Dad have!"

Second, we can bequeath to our children meaningful and significant rituals. Much of the beauty and significance of home is caught up in these family, social, national, and religious ceremonies and rituals. The Jews have been our teachers at this point. Three of their celebrations have special meaning for the family. The Passover, a family ceremony presided over by the father and

participated in by the entire family, is deeply
rooted. The Feast of Weeks is also an annual
festival that the family shares together. And the
Feast of Tabernacles was a time when, in a festival
atmosphere, the family lived in tents, temporary
booths. It was the ceremony of harvest and thanksgiving.

Now, in retirement, there is time, along with
added knowledge and understanding, to give depth
of meaning and breadth of beauty to special times
and events: Christmas, New Year, Lent, Easter,
Mother's Day, Father's Day, Thanksgiving, birth-
days, wedding anniversaries, the anniversary of the
death of a loved one, or anniversaries of outstand-
ing achievements by members of the family.

Through such ceremonies and celebrations,
we bring to the surface, and put into the stream of
life and living, thoughts and emotions that lie
dormant through reticence and inhibition. Once
these enriching emotions are brought to the surface
and given expression at these special times, it is
easier to introduce them into the ordinary,
ragamuffin days of existence.

Hodding Carter once said, "There are only
two lasting bequests we can hope to give our
children, one of these is roots; the other, wings."[2]

8
REMINISCING
(It Brings "Roses in December")

A few days ago, I reread the old Greek myth of Charon, the kindly boatman whose job it was to ferry spirits of the departed across the river Styx into the future world. The story tells of a woman who came to be carried across the river and Charon reminded her that she might drink of the waters of Leathe and forget all her past. The woman exclaimed, "I shall drink and forget all that I have suffered!" "Yes," the old boatman reminded her, "and all that you have enjoyed." "I shall drink and forget all of my failures!" "And, all of your victories," he said. "I shall drink and forget all who have hated me!" "And, all who have loved you." After a little thought, the woman entered Charon's boat without drinking the waters of forgetfulness.

But, we can choose our memories. We have that power. Our life's review need not be a photograph, an exact duplicate in which every external detail and line is recalled. Memory can be more of a painted portrait in which selected thoughts, feelings, experiences, episodes, are recalled that will give depth of meaning to the past. It does not mean that the portrait is less true than the photograph which gives the exact surface accuracy. The painted picture may be more true for it reveals something of the inner life as well as the surface appearance.

Until I retired, I was critical of the person who spent blocks of time reminiscing. I thought such a person was "living in the past" at best, and at worst was moving into a state of senility! But as a friend of mine says, "I've gotten some new light on that subject." The new light has corrected my view. I now know that there is value in reminiscing, that older people who reminisce are less depressed than those who do not. I know, too, that certain periods and experiences of life are best understood and enjoyed after they are past and from a distance of years. I have learned that reminiscing is not related to one's degree of intellectual competency, or lack of it. The learned, as well as the uninformed, are helped by remembering. A well-chosen portfolio of memories will stabilize life and give security, dignity, and a needed sense of worth. It can help a person deal with stress and is a good antidote for a guilt complex.[1]

When Philip Halsman was ready to photograph Anna Magnani, he was eager that she not be disappointed with his work, so he cautioned the actress that his lens was very sharp and would show all the lines in her face. Magnani said, "Don't hide them, I suffered too much to get them."[2]

In retirement, I have come to understand that memory builds and reveals character. There are maxims that seek to put life into a single sentence: "Clothes make the man" (and reveals the woman, some may add). "A man is what he eats." "A man is what he reads." All too simplistic, of course. But, if you say, "A man is what he remembers," you come about as close to the truth as a single sentence can state it.

Alice Freeman Palmer, distinguished president of Wellesley, reproved a student for losing her temper at another student. The corrected young woman said, "But President Palmer, would you not have been insulted by such action?" Alice Freeman Palmer replied, "I am too big to be insulted." When the philosopher Kant was hurt by a man named Lampe, Kant wrote on his notepad, "Remember to forget Lampe."

And I have learned that wise remembering aids my relations with others. The person who only remembers the unpleasant experiences of life, the injustices done him, real or imaginary, is not a pleasant person to be around. Tennyson wrote of Sir Modred:

> But, ever after, the small violence done
> Rankled and ruffled all his heart,
> As sharp wind ruffles all day long
> A little bitter pool about a stone
> On the bare coast.[3]

Medical authorities have long emphasized the importance of memories that produce quiet and harmonious spirits. We are reminded that our mental state can make us sick or well. If we remember, dwell upon, the wrong memories, we can be in danger of inducing high blood pressure, migraine headaches, heart trouble, arthritis, and possibly cancer.

What we remember about one who has died can make the difference between bitterness and gratitude, between self-pity and happiness. In *Green Winter,* Elise Maclay, portrays the relationship between a woman whose memories are wrapped in loving kindness and a "busy," but well-meaning, young therapist. The older woman speaks:

> Preserve me from the occupational therapist,
>   God.
> She means well, but I'm too busy to make
>   baskets.
> I want to relive a day in July
> When Sam and I went berrying.
> I was eighteen,
> My hair was long and thick
> And I braided it and wound it round my head
> So it wouldn't get caught on the briars,
> But when we sat down in the shade to rest
> I unpinned it and it came tumbling down,
> And Sam proposed.

I suppose it wasn't fair
To use my hair to make him fall in love with
    me,
But it turned out to be a good marriage.

                     Reminiscing-4

Oh, here she comes, the therapist, with scissors
    and paste.
Would I like to try decoupage?
"No," I say, "I haven't got time."
"Nonsense," she says, "you're going to live a
    long, long time."
That's not what I mean,
I mean that all my life I've been doing things
For people, with people, I have to catch up
On my thinking and feeling.
"Please open your eyes," the therapist says,
"You don't want to sleep the day away."
As I say, she means well,
She wants to know what I use to do,
Knit? Crochet?
Yes, I did all those things,
And cooked and cleaned
And raised five children,
And had things happen to me.
Beautiful things, terrible things,
I need to think about them,
At the time there wasn't time,
I need to sort them out,
Arrange them on the shelves of my mind.[4]

P.S. "God gave us memory that we might have
    roses in December."[5]

9
CHANCE
("Take a Holiday from Caution")

When you find that prudent people do not commend you," wrote Emerson, "adhere to your act. . . . Give your heart a holiday from caution."[1] The best time to do that is in retirement.

Of course, in conventional thinking, age and caution go together "like a horse and carriage," or like an automobile and gasoline. Age, it is thought, is a time for rest, staying at home, conserving your energy, protecting your investments; don't go out in the rain; be sure to put on your rubbers; don't forget your umbrella; be sure that you do not overexert yourself. So, runs the well-intentioned advice.

But, in fact, the retirement years may be the best time, the first time, the only time, to take a chance. Now we can dare to experiment. The children are raised, educated, married, and launched. We have proven ourselves in job, business, or profession. A definite image has been established; the road for us has been cautious and conservative. As a cartoon has it, ours is a case of "overindulging in moderation."[2]

Edgar Lee Masters has George Gray meditate upon the marble that was carved for him, a boat in harbor with sails furled. Gray says that the marble is symbolic of his life, not just his destination. For when love was offered him, he shrank from it; when sorrow came to his door, he was afraid;

ambition beckoned, but he did not dare take a chance. He said that he had always hungered for meaning in life and that finally he understood one had to lift sail and catch the winds of destiny regardless of where they might drive. He knew that such action might end in madness but life without meaning was torture and confused desire.[3]

In addition to having lived in a careful and conservative way, fulfilling the accumulated responsibilities of midolescence, there are financial considerations that indicate the retirement years as the best time to "take a holiday from caution." Through the years we hoarded and saved and invested. Now, the egg, though small, is safely in the nest. Retirement is not the time to save, it is the time to spend—not recklessly. As for safety? There is no absolute safety this side of heaven. A millionaire today, a pauper tomorrow; records have told the story often. Besides, is full safety desirable, even were it possible? Richard Armour parodied Browning's lines to read, "The last of life for which the money's made."[4]

Leave an estate for the children? It may be just what the children do not need. Remember the first line in the will, "You do not get one dime; being of sound mind we spent it all." This is not to disregard the family and loved ones; it is to say that the time has come when you can take a chance. You can say to the children, "It is time for you to get as well as beget!"

Retirement is the time when we no longer need to be frightened by the old proverb, "What is worth doing is worth doing well." That is a half-truth, at best. It would be nearer the whole truth to have it read, "What is worth doing is worth doing poorly." For if something is really worth doing, you will have to learn to do it. That will take time, practice, discipline and overall endurance. Suppose an author never submitted anything for publication until his writing had reached perfection. We would be denied every classic on the bookshelf. Will you only play golf, hunt, fish, swim, paint when you can do these things professionally? Nonsense! Think of the fun that would go out of life. There is a place for the sheer joy of play and work regardless of your proficiency, or lack of it. We amateurs must have our day. And in retirement we are no longer afraid to do something poorly. We can take that holiday from caution. And, who knows, we just might do it quite well, once we get the hang of it!

When Armand Hammer retired from business, he was near eighty. He soon became bored and began to dabble in oil. He built one of the largest corporations in the United States, the Occidental Petroleum Corporation. Alfred North Whitehead had a brilliant career as a mathematician in two fine universities: Cambridge and the University of London. Due to age, he was forced to retire. Then, Harvard University invited him to take a chance. He began a new career and became guest lecturer in philosophy. It is widely held that what Whitehead did in retirement is more significant than his early achievements at Cambridge and London Universities.

Late in life, "Miss Lillian" Carter, former President Carter's mother, joined the Peace Corps, learned a new language, served with distinction and won the affection of the people of India. There is Dr. S. I. Hayakawa, noted semanticist, and bold president of San Francisco State University during the turbulent sixties. I was his neighbor and saw him stand "eyeball-to-eyeball" with rebellious students saying, in effect, "Thus far and no farther; not another advancing rebellious step will you take at this university." The rebelling students had met their match. Then came retirement for Dr. Hayakawa. He was in his seventies. Now he serves as United States senator from California.

"One more time," in 1943 Professor Ben Dugger was forced to retire from his position as professor of botany at the University of Wisconsin. He was in good health but the university had a mandatory retirement age which Dr. Dugger had reached. Lederle Laboratories, a pharmaceutical house, hired him to do independent research. Lederle took a chance; Ben Dugger took a chance. Result? When he was seventy-three, he discovered Aureomycin. Before he died Dr. Dugger saw that discovery control more than fifty grave maladies. There was more to come, tetracycline, the most widely used broad-spectrum antibiotic in the world. Dr. Dugger died at age eighty-four. It has been estimated that he may have helped more people to live than any physician in the world. All because when he retired he took a chance.[5]

There are people whose names made the headlines. There are others who, late in life, took their chances and found satisfaction and fulfillment.

In the dim and distant past,
When life's tempo wasn't fast,
Grandma used to rock and knit,
Crochet, tat, and baby sit.

When the kids were in a jam,
They could always count on "Grama."
In the age of gracious living,
Grandma was the gal for giving.

84 Ten Good Things I Know About Retirement

Grandma now is in the gym
Exercising to keep slim;
She's off touring with the bunch,
Taking clients out to lunch.

Driving north to ski or curl,
All her days are in a whirl,
Nothing seems to stop or block her
Now that Grandma's off her rocker!

ANONYMOUS

10
GOD

(He Serves the Best Wine Last [John 2:10])

Jesus was invited to a wedding at Cana in Galilee. His mother was present, also. During the festivities, the wine ran out and his mother reported the difficulty to Jesus. She then told the servants to do whatever her son told them to do. He gave instructions and the wine was replenished. When the steward had tasted the new wine, he said to the bridegroom, "Every man serves the good wine first and when men have drunk freely, then the poor wine; but you have kept the good wine until now." The writer adds, as a sort of a postscript, "This, the first of his signs Jesus did at Cana in Galilee."[1]

The author says that this was the first *sign*. A sign is an object, a word, a picture, that points to something else. A road sign tells how far it is to the next town. The first *sign* that Jesus did records more than the wedding of two young people. It was a *sign* that pointed to something else.

The sign points to the fact that "Cana" is the world. It affirms that when we meet the requirements that were met there and then, the results that were experienced in the there and then will be known in the here and now. Christ was invited to the wedding; the wine ran out; the party went "sour"; the instructions of Jesus were followed; joy returned. The last wine was better than the first.

That is a conviction of the Christian faith. If

we invite Christ to our weddings, to all the affairs and experiences of life, if we do what he tells us to do, live according to his instructions, life will get better and better. It may get harder and harder but it will certainly get better and better.

That is true for life itself. First, there is carefree childhood, then comes exciting youth, responsible maturity, the wisdom of age and the Father's house at last. He saves "the [best] wine" for the last. Or, think of life's relationships: there are father and mother, then childhood playmates, colleagues in business, companion and spouse, and, finally, the Friend that "sticketh closer than a brother" (Prov. 18:24). The best wine is served last.

However, it is in the realm of Christian faith itself that this truth is most clearly seen. "With long life I will satisfy him, and show him my salvation."[2] Robert Browning declared.

> Our times are in his hand
> Who saith, "A whole I planned,
> Youth shows but half; trust God:
> see all, nor be afraid!"[3]

There are at least three areas of Christian faith and experience where age has a distinct advantage over youth, areas in which God serves "the best wine last." First, in our knowledge of and our experience with the *ever-present God* along the lonely roads of life. I frequently remind myself of the beautiful verse, "I will never leave thee, nor forsake thee."[4] Wonderful promise. I memorized that verse when I was a child. And, I believed it to be true; I accepted it on faith; it was in the Bible! But it was impossible for me to know that verse from experience. Now, after a half-century of trust and experience, I still "know in part," but I do "know in part." The verse states a theological truth. God never leaves those who love and trust him. "Closer is he than breathing, and nearer than hands and feet."[5] It is impossible to know that when we are young. In age we can know it from personal experience, though imperfectly. He, thereby, saves the best wine until last.

There is a second domain where age has a distinct advantage over the earlier years. It is with the *all-providing God* along the empty experiences of life. The experience of Moses is not unknown to us. God placed him in the cleft of a rock.[6] The face of Moses was covered by God's hand; so, of course, Moses could not see God as he passed. But after God passed, Moses was able to see his back, his shoulders! A quaint way of expressing a significant truth. Life comes to us with its problems, questions, sorrows, failures, disappointments, and death. As these experiences approach we cannot see God in them; no light, only darkness. But as we endure, the crisis passes. We think about the experience, meditate, and pray. Then, gradually, a bit of light begins to appear, something vaguely familiar emerges. Often, quite suddenly, we see it! We want to "wake the town and tell the people!" God was in that experience! We can see his "back."

We do need to go softly and carefully at such times and places. Let us not say that God sent the dark experience, or that he took pleasure in such an experience when it descended upon us. What we can affirm, and in age, affirm from experience, is he was with us in and through that experience. No dark hour of life can keep God from those who love and trust him, anymore than he could be kept from the dark experiences of Daniel, the Hebrew children, or Paul.[7] Such treasures of darkness the young cannot know but for the aging, it is his best wine coming last.

The third area in which age has a distinct advantage over youth is in the realm of our travels with the ever-living God along all the trials of death. Again, it is a place where one needs to go softly and quietly with humility. Yet, one cannot affirm the Christian faith without declaring the presence of the ever-living God in the times of death.

One of the great religious voices of the early part of this century was Arthur John Gossip of Scotland. He and Mrs. Gossip loved and served together through the years. Then she preceded him in death. The first Sunday back in his pulpit, following his beloved wife's death, Dr. Gossip preached a sermon that is generally ceded to be one of the really great sermons of the English language. The title of the sermon was, "When Life Tumbles in, What Then?" He said this:

> I don't think any one will challenge my right to speak today. And what I want to say is this . . . I don't think you need be afraid of life. Our hearts are very frail; and there are places where the road is very steep and very lonely. But we have a wonderful God. And, as Paul puts it, what can separate us from his love? Not death, he says immediately, pushing that aside at once as the most obvious of all impossibilities.

> No, not death. For, standing in the roar of the Jordan, cold to the heart with its dreadful chill, and very conscious of the terror of its rushing, I too, like Hopeful, can call back to you who one day in your turn will have to cross it, "Be of good cheer, my brother, I feel the bottom, and it is sound."[8]

I would like to put everything that has been affirmed in this little book within the context of the present chapter; God saves the best wine for the last. That is true when we invite Christ to the "weddings" of life, all the affairs and experiences of life, and, do whatever he tells us to do. When that is done, "I don't think you need be afraid of life." No, "trust God, see all, nor be afraid!"

NOTES

Introduction

1. Anonymous.

2. Alvin Rabushka and Bruce Jacobs, *Old Folks at Home,* Free Press (A division of Macmillan, 1980, p. 10).

3. Hugh Downs, *Thirty Dirty Lies About Old* (Niles, IL: Argus Communications, 1979), p. 117.

4. Ibid., p. 59.

5. *Old Folks at Home,* ibid., 12.

6. Morton Puner, *To the Good Long Life: What We Know About Growing Old* (New York: Universe, 1974), p. 7.

7. Mrs. Clarence Hamilton, *Your Rewarding Years* (Indianapolis: The Bobbs-Merrill Company, Inc., 1955), p. 16.

8. Garson Kanin, *It Takes a Long Time to Become Young* (Garden City, NY: Doubleday & Co., Inc., 1978), p. 142.

9. Old Portuguese saying.

Chapter 1

1. Rabbi Abraham Feinberg, from Lillian R. Dangott and Richard A. Kalish, *A Time to Enjoy* (New York: Prentice-Hall, 1979), p. 151.

2. Ibid., p. 141.

3. Howard and Charlotte Clinebell, *The Intimate Marriage* (New York: Harper & Row, 1970), p. 193.

4. Norman Cousins, *An Anatomy of an Illness* (New York: W. W. Norton & Co.).

5. Dangott and Kalish, p. 121.

6. Ibid., p. 139.

7. Garson Kanin, *It Takes a Long Time to Become Young,* Doubleday, 1978, p. 5.

8. Billie Varner, *News and Observer,* February 25, 1979, Sect. III, p. 1.

9. Dangott and Kalish, p. 140.

10. Morton Puner, *The Good Long Life: What We Know About*

Growing Old (New York: Universe, 1974), pp. 13-14.
11. Ibid., p. 140.
12. Ibid., p. 151.

Chapter 2
1. Richard Armour, *Going Like Sixty* (New York: McGraw-Hill Book Co., 1974), p. 30.
2. Peter Schwed, *Hanging in There* (Boston: Houghton Mifflin Co., 1977), pp. 44, 46.
3. *You're One in a Million, Grandpa* (Norwalk, CT: C. R. Gibson Co., 1979), no page number.

Chapter 3
1. Robert Bridges, *Selected Poems* (London: Faber and Faber, 1943), p. 52.
2. Garson Kanin, *It Takes a Long Time to Become Young* (Garden City, NY: Doubleday & Co., Inc., 1978), p. 64.
3. Barbara Cartland, *Thoughts on Love* (London: Hutchinson & Co., 1972).
4. Mrs. Clarence Hamilton, *Your Rewarding Years* (Indianapolis: The Bobbs-Merrill Co., Inc., 1955), p. 39.
5. Halford E. Luccock, *Living Without Gloves* (New York: Oxford University Press), p. 53.

Chapter 4
1. Sir William Osler, from address to Medical Library Association, Belfast, July 28, 1909.
2. Charles Lamb, *Essays of Elia,* "All Fools Day."
3. Christopher Morley, from *The Haunted Bookshop.*
4. Sir Edward Dyer, *Rawlinson Poetry,* MS 85, p. 17.
5. Kanin, p. 29.
6. John Warren Steen, *Enlarge Your World* (Nashville: Broadman Press, 1978), p. 108.
7. Izaak Walton, *The Compleat Angler.*

Chapter 5
1. G. B. Shaw, *Parents and Children.*
2. Richard Armour, *Going Like Sixty,* p. 23.
3. William Cullen Bryant, *Thanatopsis.*

4. Rudyard Kipling, "L'envoi" first stanza.

5. Dangot, p. 22.

6. Kanin, p. 115.

7. Elise Maclay, *Green Winter: Celebration of Old Age,* Reader's Digest Press, 1977, p. 5.

8. Given in a sermon on *The Lutheran Series of the Protestant Hour,* by Dr. Marshall F. Mauney, June 14, 1981.

9. Kanin, p. 101.

10. From *Fast and Slow* by John Ciardi. Copyright © 1975 by John Ciardi. Reprinted by permission of Houghton Mifflin Company.

Chapter 6

1. Laurence J. Peter, *Peter's Quotations* (West Caldwell, NJ: William Morrow and Co., 1977), p. 215.

2. William Shakespeare, Hamlet, I, 3, line 61.

3. Kahlil Gibran, *The Prophet,* "Friendship," Alfred A. Knopf, 1934, p. 64.

4. J. Winston Pearce, *Say It with Letters* (Nashville: Broadman, 1981).

5. Armour, p. 88.

6. Samuel Southard, *Like the One You Love* (Philadelphia: The Westminster Press, 1974), p. 12.

Chapter 7

1. Mrs. Clarence Hamilton, *Your Rewarding Years* (Indianapolis: The Bobbs-Merrill Co., 1955), p. 99.

2. Laurence J. Peter, *Peter's Quotations* (West Caldwell, NJ: William Morrow & Co., 1977), p. 103.

Chapter 8

1. Dangot, p. 53.

2. Kanin, p. 46.

3. Alfred Tennyson, *Guinevere,* from *The Poetic and Dramatic Works of Alfred, Lord Tennyson,* Houghton Mifflin, 1898, Lines 48-52.

4. Maclay, pp. 46-48.

5. Sir James Barrie, from Wallace Petty, *The Evening Altar* (New York: Abingdon-Cokesbury, 1940), p. 1.

Chapter 9

1. Ralph Waldo Emerson, *Emerson's Essays,* Thomas Crowell Co., 1926, "Prudence."

2. Richard Knox Smith and Sherman Goodrich, *49 and Holding,* Two Continents Publishing Group, Morgan Press, p. 141.

3. Edgar Lee Masters, *Spoon River Anthology* (New York: The Macmillan Publishing Co., 1962), p. 239.

4. Armour, p. 78.

5. *Reader's Digest,* July, 1976, 143-44, condensed from the *Miami Herald,* Jim Bishop.

Chapter 10

1. John 2:10.

2. Psalm 91:16.

3. Robert Browning, *Rabbi Ben Ezra.*

4. Hebrews 13:5*b*.

5. Alfred, Lord Tennyson, *The Higher Pantheism,* stanza 6.

6. Exodus 33:18-23.

7. Daniel 6:6; 3:6; Acts 16:24*ff.*

8. Arthur John Gossip, *The Hero in Thy Soul* (New York: Charles Scribner's Sons, 1933), pp. 109, 116.